I0147082

David O Irving

Bethel Presbyterian Church, East Orange, N.J.

An historical discourse preached at the twenty-fifth anniversary of its

organization, November 10th, 1895

David O Irving

Bethel Presbyterian Church, East Orange, N.J.
An historical discourse preached at the twenty-fifth anniversary of its organization,
November 10th, 1895

ISBN/EAN: 9783337385989

Printed in Europe, USA, Canada, Australia, Japan

Cover: Foto ©Lupo / pixelio.de

More available books at **www.hansebooks.com**

BETHEL

PRESBYTERIAN CHURCH

EAST ORANGE, N. J.

AN

HISTORICAL DISCOURSE

PREACHED AT THE

Twenty-fifth Anniversary

OF ITS ORGANIZATION

NOVEMBER 10th, 1895

BY THE

PASTOR

REV. DAVID O. IRVING

"*These temples of God's grace*
How beautiful they stand!
The honors of our native place
The bulwarks of our land."

Thistle Stationery Company
801 Broad Street
Newark, N. J.

"Ye are built upon the foundation of the Apostles
and Prophets, Jesus Christ Himself being the chief cornerstone ; in whom all the building fitly framed together
groweth unto an holy temple in the Lord."

Ephesians, ii : 20, 21.

*THERE are multitudes who go in and out,
who count the Church as theirs, who
gather from her thought, knowledge,
the comfort of good company, the sense
of safety ; and then there are others
who think they truly, as the light phrase
so deeply means, 'belong to the Church.'
They are given to it, and no compulsion could separate
them from it. They are part of its structure. They
are its pillars. Here and hereafter they can never go
out of it. Life would mean nothing to them outside
the Church of Christ."*

REV. PHILLIPS BROOKS, D.D.

Twenty-fifth Anniversary

Bethel Presbyterian Church

East Orange, N. J.

Psalm 118 15. "The voice of rejoicing and salvation is in the tabernacles of the righteous."

ANNIVERSARY occasions should be times of great joy. Songs of praise and gratitude should be heard as we celebrate our religious birthdays. Although the sorrowful is mingled with the joyful, as we regret our mistakes and mourn over the beloved fellow-workers now gone to their reward, yet we can rejoice in the Lord as we meditate upon His loving kindness and tender mercies toward our Church. This retrospect should also strengthen our trust in God as we trace His leadings and blessings, for we become more assured that He who has guided us in the past will not neglect us in the coming days. Our history can also be read for encouragement and inspiration, as we trace the humble beginnings of religious work in this community up to our present attainments. Our eyes are so often turned to the future that we sometimes forget that much can be learned from the past. Every church ought to have its history clearly and fully written so that every member may make no mistake by overlooking certain well defined facts which enter into the individual character of that particular church. As we, therefore, glance over the past and trace God's goodness in our Church's growth, may this view increase our trust in God, our regard for each other and our zeal for the future.

But let us turn the pages of our history with a sense of humility rather than of self-glory. We are not to bring before us figures and comparisons to feed our pride and conceit, for our progress has been owing to Divine grace and goodness, and not wholly dependent upon our faithfulness and zeal. God often uses the weak things of this world to confound the mighty, so that there is no need of boasting. As we become somewhat encouraged over the retrospect and prospect, let us remember our own mistakes and neglects. If we, as members of this Church, had been more faithful, liberal, devout and earnest, would we not have accomplished greater results than we now behold? But we cannot alter the past. We can only read the facts as history—"time's slavish scribe"- records them, and allow them to make their own impressions upon us.

Compared with some of the larger and more venerable churches in our vicinity, we seem to be a sort of Benjamin in the family of Israel. When we think of the one hundred and seventy-seven years of the old First Church of Orange, or the ninety-seven years which rest upon the First Presbyterian Church of Bloomfield, or the sixty-four years which belong to both the Brick Church of East Orange and the First Presbyterian Church of South Orange, we begin to realize that our twenty-five years of Church life are but a short period. But while our Church's existence may be comparatively brief, yet our Sunday school can show a considerably longer life. A review of our Church, therefore, would be incomplete without considering the history of the Sunday school. Although the latter is often called the nursery of the church, in this case "the child is father to the man," for the school is the parent of the Church. This is only one of other similar instances where churches have had their beginnings in the Sunday school. With such a fact before us we are constantly reminded of the Church's debt to the school.

Let us consider the history of

I.

THE SUNDAY SCHOOL.

I T is to the credit of this neighborhood that a Sunday school was begun as early as in other parts of Orange, and almost as soon as in other places in this country. The modern revival of the Sunday school in America dates from about the year 1816. We are told that "a local union for Sunday school work was organized in New York in 1816; another in Boston the same year, and another in Philadelphia in 1817. These societies became the nucleus of the American Sunday School Union, a national society organized in 1824."*

The earliest record we have of any religious movement of a distinctively local nature was in 1817. Only a brief account exists of the minutes of a meeting of the Sunday School Committee, as follows: "Monday evening, September 8th, 1817. The managers of the Sabbath School Society met to make arrangements for procuring books for the use of the school when it was found necessary that there should be a half dozen catechism primers and a half dozen spelling books got, which were wanted for immediate use, and four dozen religious tracts or such other books as are made use of to distribute among the children belonging to Sabbath schools as premiums. The Board authorized Mr. C. Dodd, treasurer of the society, to purchase the above mentioned books. Adjourned to meet again on Saturday evening next at seven o'clock, at the house of J. F. Crowell.

"Saturday evening, September 13th. The Board of Man-

---

* " Yale Lectures on the Sunday School," by H. C. Trumbull.

agers met and adjourned to meet again on Saturday evening next at the house of Calvin Dodd at seven o'clock."

All further record of this religious movement in this locality has been lost, but the facts have been substantiated by those who remember that there was such a school and by one who attended it, having had in his possession one of the tracts referred to above. The school was not a large one, and it was probably of a mission character. The place of meeting is not definitely known, although tradition says that it was in one of the cooper shops near our present Church. This community was then largely engaged in the manufacture of cider, and cooper shops were a necessary adjunct to the apple orchard. With our modern temperance ideas, such places would not be selected as the best in which to train the young in moral and religious truths. But people in the good old days were not so fastidious about their places of worship. The two members of the Board whose names were mentioned were Mr. Calvin Dodd, afterwards one of the first elders of this Church, and Mr. J. F. Crowell, who kept a large store on North Park street from 1813 to 1816, and for several years after had a woolen mill for fulling and carding wool, in connection with Mr. Zebina Dodd.

The reason for starting such a religious work in this place and at that time was a great revival which spread over all this part of the country. The only church then in Orange was the First Presbyterian, ministered to by Rev. Asa Hillyer, D.D. This locality was one of his preaching stations. In the Autumn and Winter of 1816 and 1817 this revival of religion spread through Newark, Elizabeth, Bloomfield, Caldwell and Orange. Dr. Hillyer was assisted in his work by two young men from Princeton, who frequently preached and held meetings for prayer in this neighborhood. One result of that revival was that the First Church organized its first Sunday school in 1817. The school in this locality was established at the same time and was probably a branch of the First Church school. How long this school continued we have no means of knowing, but it did exist for several years.

The next authentic record of any religious work of a local

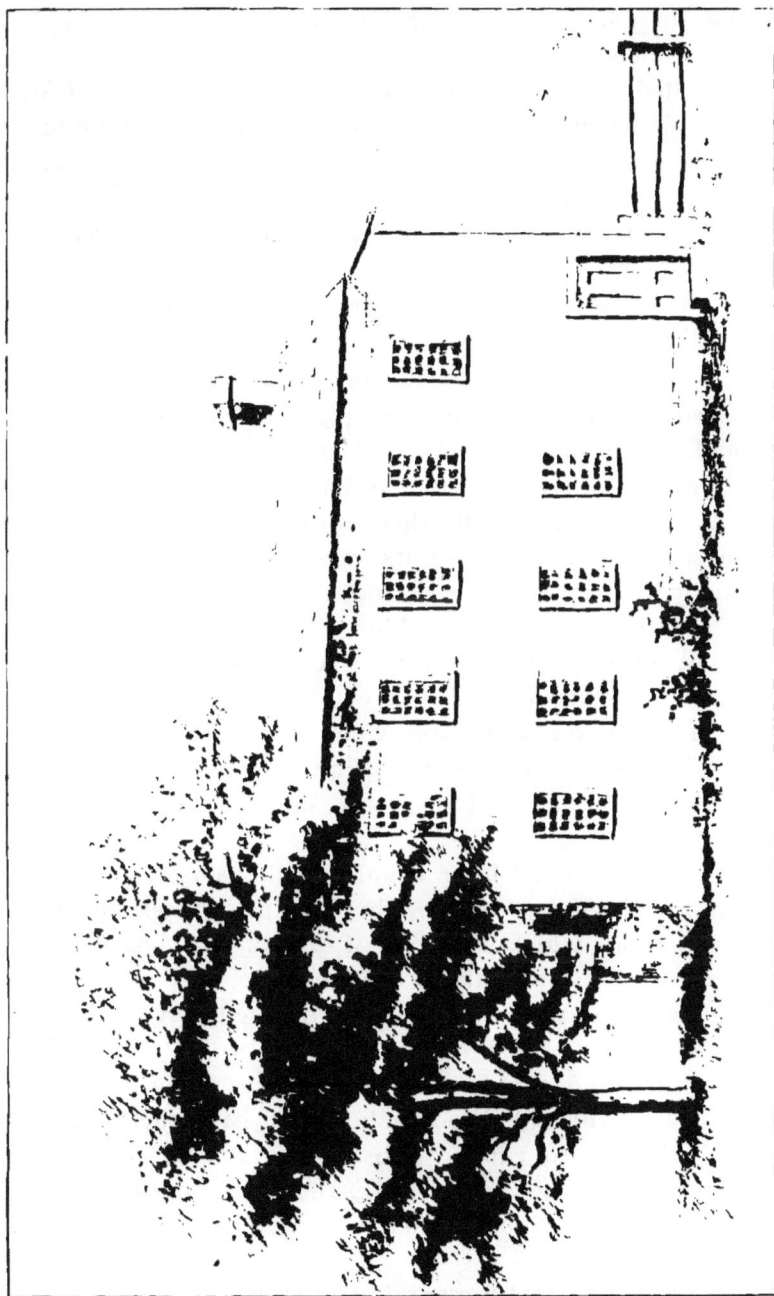

FRANKLIN SCHOOL, 1825

nature was in 1825. In the Spring of that year the people, realizing the need of a day school for the instruction of their children, called a meeting for March 13th at the house of Mr. Zebina Dodd, when the following resolutions were adopted :

"*Resolved*, That we, the subscribers, build a school house twenty feet deep by thirty-four in length and two stories high.

2. "*Resolved*, That there be seven trustees appointed to take charge of said house for the present year.

3. "*Resolved*, That the house be known by the name of the Franklin School of North Orange."*

The trustees took charge of the school April 25th, 1825, and adopted the American ten-cent piece as the common seal. The school was built during May of that same year at a cost of two hundred and thirty-three dollars and ninety-one cents. The upper room was not finished until 1832. The Sunday school used this building for its meetings and adopted its name, being known as "The Franklin Sunday School," which was afterwards changed to "The Franklin Union Sunday School." Weekly preaching services were held every Sunday and the people maintained a prayer meeting every Thursday evening. In 1830 the first Bible Class was formed, taught by Rev. Asa Hillyer, D. D., of the First Presbyterian Church, and afterwards by Rev. George Pierson, the first pastor of Brick Church.

From 1832 to 1842 John Condit Wilkinson was superintendent of the Franklin Sunday School. The services were held in the upper room, which was void of furniture, as boards were first used for seats in truly primitive style, until more comfortable ones could be provided. The people brought lath and plaster and worked at night to finish the upper room. The school also had no Sunday school library. Accordingly Mr. Wilkinson went through Bloomfield, West Bloomfield (Montclair), and Orange to raise a subscription of fifty dollars to purchase books for a library. In 1832 there was another blessed revival of religion. Special meetings were held in the old

---

* From the Book of Records and Accounts of Franklin School.

school house at five o'clock in the morning, in addition to those held in the evenings. It was a time when the cholera prevailed in New York, and Mr. Elias O. Meeker, one of the earnest workers in this place was stricken down by this dreaded disease. The work of the Holy Spirit was widely felt throughout this region and many found peace in believing in Christ.

The weekly meetings for prayer in the old school house during those years were not amidst the greatest comforts. We can borrow Emerson's description of a similar building and call it, "The old, cold, unpainted, uncarpeted meeting-house." There was a deficiency of the bright light from gas or even lamps, for every one furnished his own candle. There was no organ or piano, but the precentor, tuning fork in hand, raised the tune. They had no music books and none of our modern hymns, but the old psalms, set to metre, were freely used. We can imagine some of those prayer meetings as the little assemblage of parents and children gathers in the old school house. A dim light is cast by the flickering candles. A murmuring sound of conversation arises as neighbors interchange kind inquiries and answers. Presently the leader arises and gives out a hymn, the psalm books are brought out and the chorister, candle in hand, starts the tune. The scripture lesson is read, a few prayers are offered and exhortations are given and the meeting is dismissed. But that dingy, uninviting and dimly lighted room was often lighted by a spiritual flame. Those meetings were sources of religious power, for many earnest prayers were put up to God from that place. There souls found their Saviour, and more than one blessed season of revival was enjoyed in that room. Some of our Church's faithful workers can remember the devout meetings which were held in that old building and their lives are evidences of the good which was there accomplished. Their wishes could be truly expressed by the poet :

> " Here may we gain from Heaven
> The grace which we implore,
> And may that grace, once given,
> Be with us evermore."

The gatherings for worship were not large, as this neighborhood consisted principally of farms. Besides the inhabitants in this vicinity, some people came from Watsessing and West Bloomfield, as Montclair was then known. In 1830 the total population of Orange was only three thousand eight hundred and eighty-seven, and in 1834 it was described in Gordon's History of New Jersey as "A straggling village and post town, extending about three miles above the turnpike from Newark toward Dover, containing two Presbyterian Churches, one Episcopal and one Methodist; two taverns, ten stores, two sawmills and a bark mill, and from two hundred to two hundred and thirty dwellings, many of them very neat and commodious. A large trade is carried on in the manufacture of leather, shoes and hats." "In those days," said one of the early settlers, "Orange looked out for the head and the feet of a great part of the population. We made nothing else, but we had the satisfaction of knowing that our place was necessary for those two important points."

All record of the history of the Sunday school for a few years is lost. It probably had a changeable and fluctuating experience between the years 1842 and 1848. In the latter year Mr. David Riker assumed control as the superintendent for about four years, when, owing to lack of workers and interest, it again seemed to wane in power. The members fell off and the sessions were held only during the Summer months for a year or two. About 1854 some of the people came together again and reopened and reorganized the school. One of the workers at that time said: "We met in the upper room of the old Franklin schoolhouse and opened the school with singing, as there was no one who could open it with prayer. Soon after Mr. David Riker was elected superintendent and the school grew rapidly in numbers." Among all these teachers there was only one professing Christian, and the newly elected superintendent was the only one who was willing to pray in public. The exercises of the school, according to our modern ideas, were by no means attractive, which may account for the falling off in attendance from time to time. The services were very plain. There was no organ. In place of the bright hymns of our time the scholars sang from a psalm book several times, but always to one or at most to but few tunes. There was a monotony about the services which must have been wearisome at times even to the most zealous. Prayer was offered and a portion of Scripture read to the school. The catechism was recited, some texts of the Bible were learned, and a lesson, announced the previous week, was taught. There were no lesson helps nor Sunday school papers and a poor apology for a library; but the teachers were faithful and God blessed the feeble efforts.

The school met at half past one every Sunday until 1859 when the hour of opening was changed to two o'clock. The election of officers was held at first every three months until two years after they were chosen to hold office for six months. Under the new management the school increased rapidly in numbers and interest, until there were enrolled fourteen teachers and seventy scholars. The amount of money raised by the school at that time was between thirty and forty dollars every year.

Soon after the school was reorganized Mr. H. L. Wilson, then one of the teachers and leading workers in the cause, arranged with the different clergymen to hold preaching services every Sunday. The undenominational character of the work is seen from the list of ministers who preached in turn. They were Rev. James Hoyt, of the First Presbyterian Church; Rev. John Crowell, of Brick Church; Rev. James Williams, rector of St. Mark's Episcopal Church, and Rev. James S. Bush, of Grace Church; Rev. Mr. Freeman represented the Methodist denomination, and the Baptists were represented by Rev. Mr. Smith, of the Bloomfield Baptist Church. These ministers also organized and took charge of a weekly prayer meeting. The interior of the building was improved, and the luxury of having lamps with shades for the pulpit was obtained. About twenty dollars were raised annually from these Sunday services, but as the ministers labored without charge, the amount contributed was used to defray the current expenses needed in maintaining these religious services.

Such a spirit of unity and Christian fellowship among the

different denominations could only result in great good, so that we are not surprised to read that in 1858 a gracious revival of religion again spread over all this region. "It was a time of great financial crisis, which was spreading anxiety and gloom over the whole country." But Christians came together with one accord, to pray for the blessing. In the First Presbyterian Church a daily morning prayer meeting was held which continued from January until June. In March a union noonday prayer meeting was held by all the denominations in Willow Hall, which lasted for more than two months. The old schoolhouse in this place was also opened in which to hold these gracious meetings. On Wednesday and Friday evenings of each week and every day at noon the people came together to pour out their souls in prayer to God. All classes were reached, even the children and those indifferent to Christ's claims and calls were recipients of the blessing. The meetings were conducted quietly and without excitement. The effect was very extensive and lasting. About forty from this community, including those who had reorganized the Sunday school, united with the different churches.

The Sunday school soon after this showed its increased interest in the Lord's work by raising money for the home mission cause. For a few years between ten and fifteen dollars were contributed annually to the missionaries of the American Sunday School Union. This amount was increased until, in 1864, fifty dollars was sent to that cause. The amount of good which was accomplished at that time can be seen by referring to the many interesting letters which the missionaries sent to the school. One sum of twelve dollars was divided into two parts and used in assisting two schools in Ohio, one containing ninety and the other seventy members. "I assure you," wrote the missionary, "the donation was very acceptable. Most of the men have gone to the war, the country is new, the people are poor and the children are anxious to go to Sunday school. They made up some money among themselves and by your help they can get along quite well." Aid was given to schools in Kentucky, Michigan, West Virginia, Illinois, Indiana and other needy places in

the Home Mission field. Sometimes the gifts were used to
secure a library for some poor school, and at other times to assist
in starting a new school or to revive an old one. In many ways
these contributions from the Franklin Sunday School were blessed
by God in the destitute portions of our land. The patriotic
spirit of the school was shown in October, 1865, when twenty-
four dollars and twenty-three cents were raised as a contribution
to the National Lincoln Monument at Springfield, Illinois.

On the resignation of Mr. David Riker from the position of
superintendent, Mr. Crane was chosen to fill that office on
January 3, 1859. He remained in that position until the Autumn
of 1865, when he resigned and moved away for a time, and was
succeeded in September of that year by Mr. I. H. Gerry. In
October considerable religious interest was manifested.
"Deacon" Calvin Pierson, as he was universally called, took
a class of young men, and all in his class, consisting of eight or
ten, were converted during that revival and became earnest
Christian workers. It is fitting that special mention should be
made of this devoted seeker after souls, who, although an elder
in Brick Church, always showed considerable interest in the
religious welfare of this place. No one was more faithful in
attending the prayer meetings or in taking part in them. He
did not confine his efforts only to the religious services, but in
private conversation he would seek to press home to the hearts
of friends and acquaintances the claims of Christ. More than
one is indebted to his quiet zeal and consistent Christian life for
their entrance into the kingdom of God. This example is a
standing proof of the wide influence which a single earnest soul
can exert.

This "great revival," as it was then called, was said to have
"emanated in and from this centre." One who was present and
participated in its blessings writes : "From late in the month
of November on to the first of January, I think we never
experienced before so fully the manifest power of God's Spirit
in our midst. We were praying and laboring week after week,
holding special meetings for prayer during each week, and
notwithstanding up to the last days of the year and to the eve

of the New Year, on which we held a meeting, the room filled
with anxious souls, many deeply anxious for the salvation of
their souls and praying that God in Christ Jesus would lead
these troubled hearts to Him, yet at the close of that meeting
not a soul had expressed himself as having found the Saviour
or any relief for his burdens. We resolved to appoint a meeting
for next morning at nine o'clock. We obtained through Brother
C. D. Pierson the attendance of Rev. James H. Taylor, of the
Second Presbyterian (Brick) Church. He came over and took
charge of the meeting. We held a service of full one and a
half hour and yet it was manifest that no peace was found for a
single soul. Mr. Taylor said that we had been together a long
time and advised us all to go home to our closets, and dismissed
the meeting with the benediction. But not a person left his
seat, for every one sat down again. And now the time had
come through God's blessing when many were willing to yield
and open their hearts to the blessed Saviour who entered and
said ' Peace ' to many of those burdened hearts. Such rejoicing
as there was only a newly saved soul can experience."

One result of that revival was to lead the people to take
measures to procure a larger and more suitable building in
which to hold their Sunday school services. The school had
grown to a membership of one hundred and thirty-four. It was
the only school in the vicinity, and the time was felt to be ripe
for the erection of a building which would be devoted exclu-
sively to religious worship. Accordingly a lot was purchased, in
the Spring of 1866, from Mr. Reuben Dodd, adjoining his
residence on the west, for five hundred dollars. The Franklin
Union Sunday School was then incorporated. In June of that
year subscriptions were received for the erection of a chapel.
These were contributed mainly by the people of the district
who were interested in the movement. Some of the contributions were also given by members of other churches, of all
denominations, in Orange, but by none of the churches as an
organization. It may be well to emphasize this fact, because
the idea is prevalent in some places that the Franklin Sunday
School was a mission of the old First Church, while others have

FIRST BETHEL CHURCH BUILDING. 1866

regarded it as belonging to Brick Church. Some of its workers were prominent members of both churches, but from the first it was an independent work, and was supported wholly by local contributions. Although it was at the close of our Civil War, when everything had an inflated value, when coal could be purchased for seven dollars for half a ton, so that it was a most expensive time in which to erect a building, yet the people contributed liberally. The building cost, when completed, five thousand five hundred and twenty-two dollars and forty-three cents, which, when added to the lot, brought the total to six thousand and twenty-two dollars and forty-three cents. Of this amount about thirty-three hundred dollars were raised by subscription, about sixteen hundred dollars were the proceeds from a fair, and twelve hundred dollars mortgage was placed upon the building. The size of the structure was about fifty feet by thirty, and was considered sufficient for many years to come. Into this new building, beautiful and stately in contrast to the old, marched the school on the Sunday of its dedication. The old schoolhouse had answered its purpose, and the old had to give way to the new. But many blessed associations clustered around that dingy old building, and some now living, while more who have passed into God's kingdom above, retain sweet memories of that sacred place, where they found the Saviour and received His pardon and peace. But these hallowed places grow more blessed as time goes by, so that probably all entered the new chapel with feelings of hope and joy, while the desire for comfortable surroundings took away all regret at leaving the old building where God's Spirit so often manifested Himself. The old schoolhouse continued to be used as a public school until the new building was erected, in 1872, and it was afterwards used as the meeting place for the Congregational and the Ferry Methodist churches. It was torn down in 1891 to make way for needed improvements.

The chapel was dedicated with appropriate services in November, 1866, a number of Orange ministers being present and making short addresses. At first the infant department was held in the basement, but in 1872 an addition was built at an expense of thirteen hundred and fifty dollars, which was used by this department of the school, and also for many years by the prayer meeting, until it became too small for this purpose. The chapel was used for four years by the Franklin Union Sunday School and for twenty-one years as the place of worship for the Bethel Presbyterian Church. Probably it was not the intention of its builders to occupy it for these twenty-five years, but only to meet the needs of that time or until a church should be erected, for while it was a substantial and an eminently suitable structure, yet it was not ceiled within, nor did it have more than a small coal cellar underneath.

With the erection of this new building a change seemed to come over the character of the place. We no longer read of blessed seasons of revival. In this respect the glory of the former house was greater than that of the latter. In addition, a division of sentiment seemed to separate the workers, and instead of a strong and harmonious school an unfortunate difference arose in the community which divided the work into two factions. Without entering into the cause or justice of this division, let us read the facts as history lays them bare and consider,

II.

THE FRANKLIN DISTRICT CONGREGATIONAL CHURCH.

FOR some time a feeling had prevailed among some of the workers in the Sunday school and the inhabitants of the neighborhood that a church should be established in this place, as the nearest ones were in Orange, Brick Church and Bloomfield. This desire resulted in a meeting at the house of Mr. Calvin Dodd on the evening of May 24th, 1867, "to take into consideration the establishment of meetings for prayer and social worship by those desiring a church organization." On the thirty-first of May, at an adjourned meeting, the following preamble and resolution were unanimously adopted :

"Whereas, We, representative members of the Franklin District Community of East Orange, and members of different Christian denominations, desirous of identifying ourselves more fully with the religious interests and growth of our immediate neighborhood, and for efficiency and fellowship as workers in one common field of labor, believing that in the embodiment of the religious element in one evangelical organization upon such basis of belief as will best unite the denominations represented to be the plain dictate of Christian judgment ; therefore,

"*Resolved*, That with the blessing of God, we will form at the earliest practical moment a Congregational Church, believing that form of government best adapted to our necessities and conducive to our temporal prosperity and growth in grace."

Meetings were held at the old schoolhouse, preaching services commencing in July. On August 27th a committee was chosen to agree on "Articles of Faith, Rules of Government, and prepare a list of members desirous of uniting with the Church, and take all necessary steps to complete the organization of Church and society." A meeting was held on January 13th, 1868, when this committee made its report and presented the names of thirty persons who had brought their letters from other churches and those who were afterwards received on profession of faith. Officers were elected and Rev. Mr. Harris was chosen pastor for a year at a salary of seven hundred and eighty dollars. On the twenty-ninth of the same month an ecclesiastical council was convened to recognize the new church. The council had representatives from the Orange Valley Church; the Grove Street Church, of East Orange; the First Congregational Church, of Newark; Broadway Tabernacle, of New York city, and the New England Church, of Brooklyn. The following resolution was adopted by this council :

"*Resolved*, That having looked carefully into the history which has led to the organization of the Franklin District Congregational Church, and having examined their documents, manual, etc., we approve of their organization, and welcome this Church into the fellowship of the churches."

A public service of recognition was held on that same

evening, when a sermon was preached by Rev. M. E. Strieby and an address delivered by Rev. L. W. Bacon.

In this manner the Congregational Church was organized with Mr. Thomas Lippiatt as superintendent of its Sunday school. Mr. Gerry continued as superintendent of the Franklin Union Sunday School. This unfortunate division led to some injudicious acts which were required to be settled by the civil law .In the minutes of the Franklin Sunday School the following record appears: "The Chapel was forcibly entered on the night of the fifth or sixth of June, 1868, by some person or persons connected with the organization calling itself the Franklin District Congregational Church. The chapel was first occupied for service by the above named society on Sunday, June 21st, 1868."

The Franklin Union Sunday School therefore adjourned to the house of its superintendent and on every pleasant Sunday the school was held under the trees, until the differences between the two factions were legally settled, when the school returned to its former building. After the Congregational Church was disbanded, in time many of its members returned to the old Sunday school, and the breach eventually was healed.

Those in charge of the Congregational Church, among whom was Rev. Dr. Bacon, made overtures to the Church Extension Committee of the Presbytery to have the church taken out of the hands of the Congregational body and made over to the Presbytery. To this suggestion the Committee of Presbytery objected, fearing that some trouble might arise, but advised that the Congregational Church first disband and then allow the committee to form a Presbyterian church out of the people who, of their own will and choice, were inclined to join a Presbyterian church. This suggestion was accepted and there was accordingly formed,

THE BETHEL PRESBYTERIAN CHURCH.

A COMMITTEE of Presbytery, consisting of Rev. Eldredge Mix, D.D., of the First Presbyterian Church, of Orange; Rev. Henry F. Hickok, D.D., and Elder Calvin D. Pierson, of Brick Church, of East Orange, met in the Sunday school chapel on November 13th, 1870, and organized the Bethel Presbyterian Church, of East Orange. There were twenty-seven names enrolled,* some of whom were received from the two Presbyterian churches of Orange and East Orange, and some from the recently disbanded Congregational Church. Mr. Charles M. Davis was elected elder and Rev. James H. Marr was chosen pastor. The Sunday school property was deeded to the Presbytery, who in turn transferred the deed to the church. Trustees were elected and the organization was regularly incorporated. The name, Bethel—" House of God "—was given to the Church by the pastor, and in its acceptance by the founders and organizers of the Church, their desires for its future were best expressed : As God's house, may its name ever be kept sacred and its character always true to its name. The undertaking was begun in weakness but in great faith. It started amidst many trials and difficulties, financial and otherwise, but God's blessing rested upon that small band of followers, and He has mercifully led them through all their discouragements.

Our Church is the same age as our Presbytery. After the reunion of the old and new school branches of the Presbyterian Church in the United States of America, the several Presbyteries had to be reorganized. The churches of Orange were formerly in the Presbytery of Passaic. On June 21st, 1870, they were transferred to the new Presbytery of Morris and Orange, which held its first meeting in the First Church of Orange, July 6th. Our Church is the first one enrolled on the Presbytery's list of new churches. Since then we have seen five Presbyterian churches organized in Orange as follows : St.

* See appendix.

Cloud, of West Orange; Hillside and Orange Valley, German, of Orange; Arlington Avenue, of East Orange, and Trinity, of South Orange. There have also been the following five churches organized in our community: Washington Street and Prospect Street, Baptist; Watsessing and Ferry, Methodist, and St. Paul's, Episcopal.

At first the Church was dependent upon the Board of Home Missions for financial assistance, but through the earnest efforts of the pastor it became self-supporting, the building was refurnished, an addition was built and all its indebtedness was paid. Mr. Marr's work at first was one of laying foundations and collecting materials to build upon them. His power of organizing, which he had obtained from his experience in other similar fields, was fully called into play in his work in this locality. There were many difficulties to contend with, chief among which were the small number of workers, the changeable character of the neighborhood and the financial crisis the country passed through. All these discouragements would have wearied the heart of many another, but with his characteristic determination and perseverance Mr. Marr conquered them and was able to build up a well organized church with a large membership and a still larger Sunday school. The increase was felt the first year when the twenty-seven charter members advanced to fifty-one, and the following year to seventy-two.

The session of the Church was enlarged on January 5th, 1872, by the election of Mr. Calvin Dodd, formerly an elder in Brick Church, and Mr. Josiah F. Dodd. Mr. Calvin Dodd resigned from active service, "owing to infirmities of age," in the following year. At a Congregational meeting, held May 4th, 1875, the session was changed from the permanent to the rotary system of election and the following resolution was passed:

"In view of the wants of this, the Bethel Church, as a church of Christ,

"*Resolved*, 1st, That this Church substitute for the permanent eldership and the permanent eldership system that which is known as the rotary.

"2d, That this Church now elect three elders to serve until the annual

Respfly
Jas. H. Marr

election of officers in 1878, 1877 and 1876, as they shall themselves determine by the drawing of the lot.

"3d, That hereafter, at the annual election of officers, this Church elect anew an elder for a three years' term of service."

The elders elected were : Messrs. Ira H. Patrey, W. Irven Soverel and Charles M. Riker. In 1878 Mr. William S. Mills was elected to fill the vacancy caused by the retirement of Mr. Ira H. Patrey. In 1881 the session was increased from three to five elders by the election of Messrs. George K. Sutphen and Thomas J. Davis. The latter ceasing to act on his departure from Orange, Mr. James R. T. McCarroll was elected to fill the vacancy in 1887. The following year Mr. A. B. Spinning, formerly an elder in the New York Presbyterian Church, was added to the session, which thus increased its number to six. Mr. Herbert F. Soverel was elected in 1892 and Mr. Wm. B. Martin in 1894. Of the twelve elders who have served the Church in this capacity only two have been removed by death.

The Sunday school, under the care of the Church, its new guardian, continued to grow in numbers. At first it held a somewhat separate and independent existence, electing its own officers and transacting its own business. This it no doubt felt itself entitled to do as it had its own constitution and was entirely self-supporting. But on January 18th, 1874, it adopted its new constitution so as to bring it under the care of the Church. The preamble to that constitution reads as follows :

"Whereas, early in this century there was established in this neighborhood a Sunday school which, with a few but brief intermissions, has continued until the present time ; and

"Whereas, during this long period its name has been several times changed, and its constitution altered or altogether laid aside; and

"Whereas, the time seems to have come when its connection with the Church should be recognized, and a constitution defining its present relations and character be adopted;

"Therefore, we, the friends and teachers of the Sunday school in Doddtown, do hereby adopt the following constitution:

"Article 1. This organization shall be known by the name of the Sabbath School of the Bethel Presbyterian Church."

A still closer relation with the Church has been formed by

placing itself under the care of the session. This object was accomplished gradually and naturally. As the workers in the school and the Church became identical the interests of the two became united. As the school is considerably older than the Church it has maintained its seniority by being the larger body. It is hoped that the two bodies will become still more closely bound together so that more of the scholars may identify themselves with the Church, and that the Church will take upon itself the entire financial support of the school. A great power for good lies within the reach of this branch of the Church and it should be worked with the best of modern appliances and methods. Already the infant department has had to be divided so as to form in addition an intermediate room. The total membership of the school at last report was three hundred and ninety-seven. It has been a great blessing to the Church and community, but we should not rest satisfied with what has been done, but press on with greater hopes to new attainments.

After having served this Church faithfully and zealously for more than eleven years, Mr. Marr resigned his charge January, 1882, to accept a larger and more promising field in the Kensington district of Philadelphia. During that time he had been instrumental in raising the membership from twenty-seven to one hundred and sixty-five. The Sunday school also increased under his leadership and care to two hundred members. As the first pastor, he worked hard to contribute to the Church's success. He has laid the foundation and another is privileged to build thereupon.

The Church was left without a pastor for four months, when it called Rev. David O. Irving, then just leaving Princeton Theological Seminary. The call was accepted and the ordination and installation services took place on May 2d, 1882, under the charge of the Presbytery of Morris and Orange. Rev. Thomas Carter, of Boonton, the moderator of the Presbytery, presided and propounded the constitutional questions. The sermon was preached by Rev. Alfred Yeomans, D.D., pastor of the Central Presbyterian Church, of Orange, from the text, John 15:16: " I have chosen you and ordained you, that ye should go

30

Yrs. Sincerely
David O Irving

and bring forth fruit, and that your fruit should remain." Rev. David Irving, D.D., delivered a charge full of feeling and tenderness to the pastor. Rev. James H. Marr delivered a loving and earnest charge to the people. It is very startling to know that all of those ministers who took part in that service have been called home to a service above.

For a few years the growth of the Church was slow, owing to the stationary condition of the neighborhood. Gradually, as local improvements increased, the people began to move into this neighborhood, and the Church felt the change. New workers often meant new work. Societies were organized and set at work. The Ladies' Aid Society was started in 1885, which raised funds to paint and paper the interior of the building, to procure reflectors whereby gas could be used as an illuminator in place of oil, to purchase a larger organ, and to meet the expenses connected with the Christmas entertainments for the Sunday school. A Young Ladies' Missionary Society was organized in February, 1888, which has increased an interest in the cause of Home and Foreign Missions, and which has sent contributions of money and clothing to those in destitute parts of the world. This organization also seeks to train the younger girls, and it has charge of the Band of Willing Aids. Another society, somewhat similar in aim, but which seeks to help those nearer home, was started on November 26th, 1889, and was called the Ladies' Home Missionary Society. Money and boxes of clothing have been given to local charitable institutions, to the poor of New York city, and to many a needy Home Missionary family. The need of reaching and training the young people was felt, and a Christian Endeavor Society was formed on December 5th, 1890. It has grown from its fourteen charter members to fifty-two active, twenty associate and three honorary members. Its three committees at its organization have increased till they number seven. More than twenty of its members have united with the Church during the history of the society. Flowers are sent every week during the Summer to the Flower Mission, of New York city, and money is contributed annually to missions. On December 8th, 1892, a Junior Christian Endeavor Society was formed, which holds weekly meetings except during the three Summer months. Starting with twenty-three members, it has grown to sixty. These children are taught the need of giving to those in poverty and want, and of taking a deep interest in the work of missions at home and abroad, and they have early shown their benevolent spirit.

In glancing over the work of the Church for the last twenty-five years we may find some facts to encourage us even if we record them in no boastful feeling but in the spirit of humility. Looking first at the financial condition of the Church we note that there has been contributed for all purposes about one hundred thousand dollars. Of this amount the benevolent column shows a total of about eight thousand four hundred and fifty dollars. After all, the benevolent column of the finances of the Church is the most important of all, as benevolence is the true kind of giving. It is disinterested and shows the love which we bear to Christ and His needy ones. While the benevolent gifts of our Church cannot compare with those of larger and more wealthy churches, yet it is not a discreditable showing when we consider that for many years the Church had to struggle with adversities and financial embarrassments, while its membership was for a long time very small. Many of the societies have been in existence but a few years, so that their contributions do not increase the total amount as much as they otherwise would. The figures given above represent not the gifts of the wealthy, but of those in moderate circum-stances who give with self-denial. But God accepts and uses the gifts of those who contribute in this manner. Let this benevolent statement be only a beginning which the Church will be able largely to surpass at its next quarter of a century celebration.

The Church has raised for its own expenses over ninety thousand dollars. It is not within the power of human reason to decide whether the amount of good accomplished in the individual souls and in the community is a full value for the money expended. God does not keep His records on the same system of book-keeping as we are apt to do. But it is

to be hoped that the money thus put into the Church treasury
has been wisely and judiciously expended so as to have a
moral and benevolent effect upon the community. A considerable amount of this money has been expended in the
erection of our present building, whose fourth anniversary
we celebrate at this same time.

Feeling the need of more accommodation than our other
building afforded, an effort was made in 1886 to collect money
to build a larger and more commodious structure. The necessity
for more room and more convenient accommodations compelled
the officers to take steps towards the securing of funds for the
erection of a better building in which to worship God. The
first contribution was fifty-seven dollars, the proceeds of an
entertainment. In many little ways this amount was increased.
Some smiled at these feeble efforts and predicted that many
years would elapse before sufficient money would be collected
to warrant the starting of a church edifice, while they offered
no hopes about any large and substantial structure. But others,
whose faith was greater, despised not the day of small things,
but trusting in God and putting forth their own efforts, looked
for grand results, and, as in all cases the people of faith and
effort, were able to see their hopes realized.

Through the generosity of Mr Josiah F. Dodd, a valuable
plot of ground on the northwest corner of Dodd Street and
Midland Avenue, consisting of seventy-five feet by one hundred
and twenty-five feet, was given to the Church. As this was
more suitable for a large edifice than the former Church lot,
the gift was gladly accepted, while it added a stimulus to the
workers and seemed to make the scheme more real and tangible
to the faint-hearted. Afterwards the lot was increased by a
further donation of twenty-five feet on Dodd Street, while
twenty-five feet additional on Midland Avenue was purchased
for four hundred dollars. This amount was raised by private
subscriptions on the part of the Building Committee. The
work was still further aided by the generous contribution of
a friend, whose name must be held by request, of two thousand
dollars. This gift was appreciated for itself and the good

35

wish of the giver, and also because it was received at just the right opportunity to encourage all those who had the work of the new Church at heart. We felt that we were not working alone, but that God was raising up generous friends of the enterprise. A Building Committee was elected at a meeting of the parish on January, 1890. It consisted of the board of trustees and four members from the congregation, as follows : Messrs. Wm. S. Mills, Jas. R. T. McCarroll, H. B. Thistle and the pastor. It immediately set to work to select an architect and plans. Mr. Isaac Pursell, of Philadelphia, was chosen, and the plan of a stone building adopted, costing, exclusive of furnishings and windows, twenty-three thousand dollars.

Work was begun on the new Church on Monday, July 21st, 1890, when Rev. James H. Marr, in the pastor's absence, formally turned the first spadeful of earth for the excavation of the foundation. The corner-stone was laid on Wednesday, September 17th, at five o'clock in the afternoon. As the day was stormy it was feared that the services would have to be held under cover. But the rain having ceased for a time it was decided to brave the elements and have all of the exercises at the place where the cornerstone was to be laid. Accordingly the procession formed at the old Church and marched to the new site on Midland Avenue. The pastor led with the invited clergy. After them came the members of the session, deacons, trustees and building committee. They were followed by the older members of the Church and of the congregation and by the children of the Sunday school. The procession wound around to the rear of the Church and passed on the temporary floor to the front of the Church. The ceremonies had hardly begun before the rain began to fall and the services were held underneath umbrellas. However, the rain did not dampen the spirits of the worshipers. The services opened with a prayer of invocation by the Rev. Henry F. Hickok, D.D., of Brick Church, East Orange, and the doxology was sung by the congregation. The Scripture lesson from 1st Corinthians, 3d chapter, beginning with the ninth verse, was read by Rev. Stanley White, of the Hillside Presbyterian Church, of Orange.

The cornerstone hymn was then sung to the tune of Hebron, as follows:

"An earthly temple here we raise,
Lord God, our Saviour! to thy praise;
Oh, make thy gracious presence known
While now we lay its cornerstone.

"Within the house thy servants rear
Deign by thy Spirit to appear;
On all its walls salvation write,
From cornerstone to topmost height.

"And when this temple, "made with hands,"
Upon its firm foundation stands,
Oh, may we all with loving heart
In nobler building bear a part,

"When every polished stone shall be
A human soul won back to thee;
All resting upon Christ above,
The chief and precious cornerstone.

"So when our toil is o'er at last,
All labor in both temples passed,
Oh, may it then by works be shown
That faith hath laid this cornerstone."

At the close of this hymn, Mr. William S. Mills, chairman of the building committee, read a list of the contents of the box, which were as follows: The Holy Bible; the Confession of Faith; an historical record of Bethel Church; a list of members at the organization of the Church; a list of members of the Church, September 17th, 1890; the names of the officers of the Church and officers, teachers and scholars of the Sunday school; the names of the architect and contractors; pictures of the old Church and of the old Franklin Schoolhouse; coins of 1890; copies of the Orange *Chronicle, Journal, Herald, Volksbote* and Evening *Mail*, the East Orange *Gazette*, the Newark *Advertiser, News* and *Journal*, the New York *Times, Tribune* and *Herald*, the *Church at Home and Abroad* for September, 1890, the *Christian at Work* for September 11th, 1890; copies of the

Confession and Covenant of Bethel Church, the year text and prayer meeting topics for 1890, the annual report for 1889 and the programme of the order of services of laying of cornerstone.

After the stone had been placed in position by the workmen the pastor formally pronounced the stone laid, using a silver trowel, which was provided for the occasion. A prayer of thanksgiving and dedication was then offered by Rev. George A. Paull, pastor of the Westminster Presbyterian Church, of Bloomfield. After the congregation had sung one verse of the hymn, "Holy, holy, holy, Lord, God Almighty," the benediction was pronounced by Rev. William F. Whitaker, pastor of the St. Cloud Presbyterian Church, of West Orange. On the following Sunday a sermon appropriate to the occasion was preached by the pastor.

The new building was completed in November, 1891. The interest in its success may be judged from the special donations which were given. Three large and handsome memorial windows were donated, as follows: The East Window, representing Elijah fed by the ravens, was a memorial to Mr. Calvin Dodd, one of the first elders of the Church, a gift of Mrs. Amzi Dodd. The South Window represents Faith, and was in memory of Mrs. Hannah Condit Dodd. It was donated by Mr. Samual Dodd, of St. Louis, Mo. The West Window, containing the symbols of the Cross and Alpha and Omega, was a memorial to Rev. David Irving, D.D., a gift of Mrs. Elizabeth F. Irving and Rev. David O. Irving. A smaller window on the west represents a dove and was in memory of Mrs. Martha Tucker, for many years one of our members, and was a gift of members of her family. The steam heating was a donation of Mr. Amzi T. Dodd. The Sunday school contributed the bell and furnished their own school room. A class of young men provided the pulpit and communion furniture, suggesting that the pulpit should always keep in touch with the young. The Ladies' Aid Society furnished the pews and carpet in the Church and the Young Ladies' Missionary Society donated the cathedral glass windows in the Sunday school room. The organ was the

INTERIOR OF NEW CHURCH

gift of a few of the members who agreed to raise the necessary funds to secure it.

On Sunday, November 1st, 1891, farewell services were held in the old Church building before a crowded audience. The services in the morning consisted of reminiscences, and in the evening a bright and hopeful outlook, under the guidance of God's Spirit, was set forth. In the afternoon the Sunday school was addressed by the superintendent, pastor and teachers. On Tuesday evening of that week the last prayer meeting was held in "the place where prayer was wont to be made." It was a meeting full of tender recollections, blessed associations and hopeful anticipations. Testimonies from this one and that one who had been born into the kingdom of God in that place were feelingly given.

The dedication Sabbath, November 8th, was a bright and beautiful one, and the new building was crowded by the regular members of the congregation, former members, and friends of the Church. The services opened with the singing of the doxology, which was followed by the prayer of invocation and the Lord's Prayer. The hymn "Holy, holy, holy, Lord, God Almighty," was then sung by the congregation. A specially prepared Scripture lesson was then read responsively. The prayer of dedication was then offered by the pastor. After singing the hymn beginning, "O Thou whose own vast temple stands," the sermon was preached by Rev. M. W. Jacobus, professor in the Hartford Theological Seminary. The dedication offerings were then collected, and the services closed with the familiar hymn, "All hail the power of Jesus' name."

In the afternoon the Sunday school held a special service, which was largely attended. The school met at half-past two in the Sunday school room, where two hymns were sung and a prayer dedicating that room to Almighty God was offered by the superintendent, Mr. William S. Mills. The school then marched into the Church where they were addressed by Mr. David L. Wallace, superintendent of the Central Church Sunday school, of Orange ; Mr. Silas M. Giddings, president of the Brooklyn Sunday School Union ; and Rev.

James H. Marr, pastor of the Beacon Presbyterian Church, of Philadelphia.

In the evening the Christian Endeavor Society held a short service, and in the Church another large congregation gathered to hear Rev. Mr. Marr, the former pastor, preach. On Monday evening a service of welcome was held when addresses by the following Presbyterian pastors of the Oranges were made: Rev. Henry M. Storrs, D.D., of the First Church of Orange; Rev. Henry F. Hickok, D.D., of Brick Church; Rev. James M. Ludlow, D.D., of First Church of East Orange; Rev. William F. Whitaker, of St. Cloud; Rev. Stanley White, of Hillside avenue; and Rev. S. J. McClenaghan, of Elmwood Mission. A letter of congratulation was read from Rev. Rufus S. Green, D.D., who was detained at home by illness. On Tuesday evening a very earnest prayer meeting was held, the first in the new Church. On the following evening another service of welcome was held when addresses were delivered by Rev. E. D. Clough, of the Washington Street Baptist Church; Rev. Mr. Clement, of the Watsessing M. E. Church; and Rev. Mr. Kemble, of the Ferry Methodist Church. Letters of regret were read from Rev. F. W. Baldwin, of the Trinity Congregational Church and Rev. Mr. Dickinson, of the North Orange Baptist Church.

The following Sabbath was observed as a sacramental one, when we welcomed into our number eight on profession of their faith in their Saviour and nine by letter from other churches. In this manner we entered upon the larger work in our new building, praising God for His goodness and relying upon Him for His help and guidance. The prayer and desire of many could be well expressed by the poet Bryant:

> " May faith grow firm and love grow warm
> And pure devotion rise,
> While round these hallowed walls the storm
> Of earth-born passion dies."

In moving into our new edifice we incurred a larger debt than we had hoped to carry, owing to the failure of some funds we were led to expect to receive. But the people nobly shouldered the burden of seventeen thousand dollars, and by the realization of three thousand and five hundred dollars from the sale of our old lot and building and by the aid of the Debt Lifting League we have been able to reduce this amount by more than one-half, and we are led to believe that the remainder will soon be wiped out as one practical result of our twenty-fifth anniversary. The load was at first very difficult to carry, as we all felt the recent depression of the times, while the rate of interest to be paid was unexpectedly increased. But the Lord stood by us and we render all the glory to Him. With a smaller financial burden to carry we will be able to bear a larger share of our responsibility in the work of the Universal Church in extending the cause of Christ throughout the world.

In glancing at the spiritual history of the Church we can rejoice that we have been making some progress through the blessing of God upon our efforts. The original twenty-seven members have increased to three hundred and twenty. There has been received into membership since the organization of the Church a total of four hundred and seventy-seven. Two hundred and twenty-four of these on profession of faith in Christ and two hundred and fifty-three by letter from other churches. We have lost by death thirty-one and by removals one hundred and twenty-six. Our growth has been gradual rather than rapid. There has been only one season of revival during the twenty-five years, and that was in 1893. At that time our Church united with other churches of East Orange in the evangelistic services held in the Munn Avenue Presbyterian Church from November 6th to 13th, under the direction of Rev. B. Fay Mills. These meetings were productive of great blessings. As a result of those special services, we received twenty-five into our fellowship on profession of their faith in Jesus Christ, many of whom were representatives of the young people. But we cannot tabulate in figures the spiritual benefits derived in the deepening of the religious feeling, the quickening of Christian zeal and the awakening of the individual conscience, showing that God's Spirit was at work in our midst. Those who

43

were present at the prayer meetings, held in our lecture room the week after the general meetings were finished, probably will never efface from their memories the delightfully solemn impressions then made, as night after night for three weeks the people crowded into the room of prayer and consecration. All other engagements were given up for those evenings and little else could be talked about during those days. One very hopeful and interesting feature of the work was the effect it had upon the young, especially in the Sunday school. Sabbath, November 12th, was a day of religious interest, when one hundred and twenty-two scholars signed cards signifying their desire to become Christians or to lead a more consecrated life. Nor did the work stop here, for the influence of these children was felt in the home, and parents were brought to the Saviour, thus confirming the words of Scripture, that " a litttle child shall lead them."

While this has been the only revival to record since our Church was organized, yet it would be unfair to draw any lesson from it showing lack of zeal for the welfare of souls or want of desire for the presence of God's power. The Holy Spirit, like the wind, cannot be directed whence He cometh nor whither He goeth. Many faithful ones have been praying and working for the salvation of souls, and their history is written by the Heavenly Historian in the records on high. So far as their influence has been felt in the history of our Church we can only describe it in a general way. But their prayers and faithful efforts have helped in many ways to keep alive the spiritual interests of the Church, while the lack of the outpouring of the spiritual blessings upon us has been a source of sorrow to them.

One evidence of the Holy Spirit's blessing may be seen in the increased interest taken in the subject of missions. Not only by our gifts is this interest to be measured, but by the growth of the missionary societies and their increased work. Even the young in the Sunday school and in their various societies have felt the claims of the needy upon them. By their reading, their different missionary meetings and their wide-awake interest in returned missionaries, many have proved that this cause is

INTERIOR OF OLD CHURCH

becoming dearer to their hearts. While this spirit is not as active nor as extensive as some of us would like, yet its growth is a cause for congratulation and a hope of a brighter future. While we give of our means to the cause of missions, let us also give ourselves to this great work of evangelizing the world. In all our Church's history we cannot record the name of a single missionary who has gone out from our midst. Let this past neglect be more than met in coming years by the consecration of many earnest souls for the Lord's work in foreign lands. In fact we have but one from our membership who has gone out to preach the gospel, the Rev. Samuel Warrender, who united with the Church September 2d, 1873. If parents would only consecrate their children to this work of the Church and seek to influence them in this direction the coming years would show a greater gain in the missionary spirit and missionary work. Our Church is sufficiently strong and large to be personally represented on many of the mission fields of the world.

> " We sow in tears ; but let us keep
> Our faith in Christ and trust Him still ;
> Yonder our harvest we shall reap,
> Where gladness every heart shall fill."

In glancing forward we should see our needs so as to meet them as speedily as possible, and hold out hopes so as to fulfill them as ambitiously and earnestly as we can, relying wholly upon Divine grace and guidance. But it may not be amiss to refer to a few points upon which we can improve.

1. We should seek as soon as possible to pay off all of our indebtedness. This we can do if we earnestly and consecratedly set ourselves to do it. This we ought to do for our own temporal and spiritual good, and for the benefit which we can render to others. We have been enabled to reduce the mortgage more than one-half since we started four years ago and with faith and effort we will soon see it vanish entirely, leaving us free to do greater work for the Lord.

2. The Church should support its own Sunday school. Our circumstances and history make the relation of the school

to the Church rather unusual, but the Church is now strong enough financially to care for the school. This would be only about one hundred dollars additional every year and it would leave the school free to train the scholars in the work of benevolence. Perhaps the Sunday school would then be able to undertake by itself to erect a larger and more suitable bu lding in which to hold its sessions. Already the infant department is obliged to meet in the old Church on account of its crowded condition, and other parts of the school give an indication that larger accommodations will soon be needed. It has been suggested that a more commodious structure of wood be erected on the property adjoining the present building on the north for the Sunday school and that the rooms we already have be used for the prayer meetings of the different societies, as well as for all social meetings of the Church. It is hoped that this suggestion may meet with favor and that some practical means of carrying it out may soon be found. The important work of our Church has always been the Sunday school, and this department should not be overlooked. In our Sunday school work we should keep in touch with the more advanced educational ideas and we should use the most approved methods to make that branch of the Church the most successful.

3. It may be a question for us to decide in the future whether we should seek to make our work more of the nature of an institutional church and, if so, to what extent. We have always maintained the voluntary system of support so that none need feel that they are too poor to come to God's house. We want them to feel at home with us and we should strive to make them feel at home in our Bethel. Providence has given to us a grand opportunity and we should not refuse to accept God's leadings. With a free library and reading-room open every week-day evening, where many could go, who have now no place to resort which is elevating, we might be able to reach many careless ones who would not be attracted to our religious services. A sewing class for the children of the poor would prove a blessing to many a needy home. The employment of a Bible reader to bring the story of Jesus and His love into many

a neglected household would be another instrument in the hands of God of reaching and saving souls, besides brightening their homes. Let no one think that these ideas are visionary, for if the Lord opens the way let our faith and courage be strong enough to follow.

4. A last suggestion could be given about the developing and training of children for the ministerial and missionary life. Our Church is large enough to have many workers on the field. But parents must consecrate their children when young to this service and bring them up with earnest and believing prayers for such a work. Let there be a deepening of spiritual life and a quickening of faith in God and an arousing of love for souls and then there will be many pressing into the ministry, saying, "Woe is me if I preach not the Gospel of Christ."

May this prospect cheer and encourage, arouse and enkindle all in this Bethel to come to the help of the Lord in this place, while the retrospect may increase our faith as it shows how much can be done when there is united effort, even if it is by the comparatively humble and feeble exertions.

NAMES OF THE MEMBERS WHO JOINED BETHEL CHURCH AT ITS ORGANIZATION, NOVEMBER 13TH, 1870:

CALVIN DODD,*
JOSIAH F. DODD,*
ELEANOR DODD,
DAVID HUNTER,*
MARGARET HUNTER,*
ELIZA HUNTER,
MARGARET McLANE,*
SARAH McLANE,
SARAH A. RAY,
PHEBE VAN ORDEN,*
ALEXANDER HUNTER,†
ANNIE HUNTER,†
ELIZA DODD, SR.,*

ELIZA DODD, JR.,†
NANCY M. DODD,*
SARAH S. DOWNS,
MARY E. DOWNS,
PETER S. VINCENT,†
ELIZA L. VINCENT,†
JULIA VINCENT,
WILLIAM S. VINCENT,†
WILLIAM S. MILLS,
ELIZABETH MILLS,*
ISRAEL DODD,
ANGELINE DODD,
ANNA M. TAYLOR,†

CHARLES M. DAVIS.†

* Deceased.
† Dismissed to other churches.

ELDERS OF BETHEL CHURCH.

	ELECTED.		CEASED TO ACT.
CHARLES M. DAVIS	November	20th, 1870	1875
CALVIN DODD	January	5th, 1872	1874
JOSIAH F. DODD	January	5th, 1872	1875
IRA H. PATREY	May	4th, 1875	1878
W. IRVEN SOVEREL	May	4th, 1875	
CHARLES M. RIKER	May	4th, 1875	
WILLIAM S. MILLS	January	8th, 1878	
GEORGE K. SUTPHEN	January	11th, 1881	1892
JAMES R. T. McCARROLL	January	12th, 1887	December 8th, 1892
A. B. SPINNING	January	13th, 1888	
HERBERT F. SOVEREL	January,	1892	
WILLIAM B. MARTIN	April,	11th, 1893	

DEACONS OF BETHEL CHURCH.

	ELECTED.		CEASED TO ACT.
CALEB RIKER	January	5th, 1872	1876
CHARLES M. RIKER	January	5th, 1872	1878
ALEXANDER HUNTER	January	5th, 1872	1874
WILLIAM S. MILLS	January	11th, 1874	1880
IRA DODD	January	11th, 1876	1879
LEWIS SMITH, SR.*	January	8th, 1878	
JAMES GILMOUR	January	14th, 1879	1891
W. W. WESTERVELT	January	12th, 1880	1883
IRA H. PATREY	January	9th, 1883	1887
GEORGE M. TYLER	March,	1887	
HENRY SMITH	March,	1887	
HERBERT F. SOVEREL	January	15th, 1891	1894
GEORGE B. HIGINBOTHAM	January	17th, 1894	

* Died February 7th, 1892.

TRUSTEES OF BETHEL CHURCH.

	ELECTED.	CEASED TO ACT.
NICHOLAS ALBEY ... . January	13th, 1874	1877
W. I. SOVEREL .... January	13th, 1874	1891
LEWIS SMITH, JR.......... .... January	13th, 1874	1877
HENRY SMITH............... January	13th, 1874	1877
IRA PATREY .... January	13th, 1874	1876
ALEXANDER HUNTER .. .. January	11th, 1876	1877
THOMAS WALKER .... January	9th, 1877	
GEORGE H. KUTCHER........ January	9th, 1877	
W. M. VAN NESS... .. .. January	9th, 1877	1889
CALEB RIKER .. .. January	9th, 1877	1879
JAMES GILMOUR............ January	8th, 1879	1881
BENJAMIN PARKHURST...... January	11th, 1881	1888
CHARLES M. WHITLOCK .... January	11th, 1888	1890
STEPHEN W. HERDMAN..... January	11th, 1888	1889
FLETCHER PLACE, JR .. January	16th, 1889	1895
SILAS W. DODD............ January	16th, 1889	
GEORGE LAW...... .... January	15th, 1891	1894
JOHN H. MOORE .... January	15th, 1891	
DAVID W. BALL .... January	17th, 1894	
H. A. HICKOK .... January	17th, 1895	

SUNDAY SCHOOL SUPERINTENDENTS

JOHN CONDIT WILKINSON........ 1832	1842
DAVID RIKER 1848	1859
CHARLES CRANE.................... 1859	1865
I. H. GERRY 1865	1871
CHARLES M. DAVIS...................... ..1871	1873
JAMES GILMOUR...................... .. .1873 (January to June.)
CHARLES M. DAVIS...... ....1873 (June.)	1875
REV. JAMES H. MARR 1875	1882
THOMAS J. DAVIS................. 1882	1884
WILLIAM S. MILLS..... 1884	1893
WILLIAM B. MARTIN................... .. 1893	1894
WILLIAM S. MILLS 1894	1896

YEAR TEXTS.

1886 "Let us put on the armour of light." Roms. 13:12.

1887 "Holding forth the Word of life." Phil. 2:16.

1888 "Who went about doing good." Acts 10:38.

1889 "Follow me and I will make you fishers of men." Matt. 4:19.

1890 "Christ in you the hope of glory." Col. 1:27.

1891 "For other foundation can no man lay than that is laid, which is Jesus Christ." 1 Cor. 3:11.

1892 "Walk as children of light." Eph. 5:8.

1893 "Who shall separate us from the love of Christ." Roms. 8:35.

1894 "Yield yourselves unto God, as those that are alive from the dead." Roms. 6:13.

1895 "All things are possible to him that believeth." Mark 9:23.

51

BIOGRAPHICAL NOTICE

REV. JAMES H. MARR.

James Hervey Marr was born in Lewisburg, Pa., April 3d, 1842. His father, Rev. P. B. Marr, was pastor of the Presbyterian Church of that place. He thus came from a ministerial family, as not only his father, but also his grandfather on his mother's side, had served the Lord in that capacity. The unfeigned faith of the parents was thus transmitted to the son. It was only natural that he should have inherited the taste, as well as the right, for the gospel ministry, having descended from such godly ancestors and reared amidst such sacred influences. Having been early given to the Lord by these parents, the Heavenly Father accepted the gift and shaped his course so that he could be useful in his chosen field.

One who knew him well has written about his early life in these words : " His mother had often remarked that original sin showed itself before a child was six months old. She had made it the rule to repress the evil from infancy, and, though he was the fourth child, she had never failed in bringing the youthful rebels under control at an early period. When James was to be subjugated she found a difficult problem on hand, as he scarcely knew how to yield. She was perplexed, and expressed her alarm to an experienced friend, who told her that the strong will might be a source of great good ; that she should rely on prayer and the good example of the older children to bring the boy into the paths of righteousness. It seemed to her a dangerous experiment, but she waited. The early tendencies of the boy were in the main correct. He showed an indomitable energy and unyielding determination in everything he undertook. He dug and planted a large garden at some distance from home, often rising at four in the morning to carry on the task outside of shady hours, and in due season he had the satisfaction of turning in a quota to the family support. It was a household of activity and he was ready to bear his part of the burden.*

"He entered the University of Lewisburg and completed his course in 1860. Graduating when only seventeen years old, the youngest in his class, he took the first honors. He then entered the junior class of Princeton College from which he was graduated in 1862. He soon had a high position in his class there, though making his support largely from his own exertions. After leaving college he entered the Princeton Theological Seminary. When he graduated in the Class of 1865 he was well equipped for a scholarly life in some settled pastorate in the East. The German and French tongues were at his command as well as the classic. It was his habit early in his ministry to read a chapter in the Bible each day of the week in different languages."

After he was licensed to preach the gospel he spent a short time in Baltimore as a stated supply, then a few months in Central Pennsylvania. Like the great apostle, he sought to avoid building upon another man's foundation. The needs of the West then opening for the farmer, miner and pioneer, called him to bear the standard of the cross to those destitute portions. Accordingly, in 1866, he settled in Minnesota as a home missionary, and established the three churches at La Crescent, Hokah and Brownsville. Blessed by nature with a strong and wiry constitution, he was not afraid of hard work, and his willingness in this respect often had an opportunity to exercise itself in those frontier towns.

The next year he proceeded to San Francisco. His trip to California was a specimen of his daring and energy. He fretted under the slow progress made by the caravan through Texas, and taking a large mule as his only aid and companion, he started

---

* "G," in *The Presbyterian*, June 10th, 1865.

on ahead to ferret out the way through New Mexico, Arizona and Southern California. He traveled by night to escape the murderous Indian, and sought obscure retreats during the day. He joined the Presbytery of San Francisco and was ordained as an evangelist on the twenty-first of March, 1868. He established the Howard Street Church of that city and remained as its stated supply until 1869, when feeling that his enterprise there was well established he turned toward the East. His return was waited for by his parents with eager longing. His first token of filial affection and old-time solicitude for his mother's comfort was shown by handing her out of his scant savings a hundred dollars in gold which a kind friend had given him as he departed from the land of gold.

In the Summer of 1870 he settled in East Orange, and when the Bethel Presbyterian Church was organized in November of that year he was chosen as the stated supply. The name "Bethel" was suggested by him, and that name will always be a benediction from him since he has gone home to worship God in the Heavenly Bethel, "the house not made with hands, eternal in the Heavens."

The discouragements of the new undertaking would have wearied the heart of many another minister, but Mr. Marr, with his characteristic determination and perseverance, conquered all of these difficulties and built up a strong and well organized church, free of all indebtedness, with a large membership and a still larger Sunday school. Many of the poor and needy of the community, whether members of the Church or not, felt the influence of his self-denying and persistent labor.

After having served this Church for more than eleven years, he departed in January, 1882, to become the pastor of the Cumberland Street Presbyterian Church in the Kensington district of Philadelphia. That church had greatly run down, but his organizing force was largely felt in its upbuilding. The next year the name of the church was changed to the Chandler Memorial Church, and in 1886 it was again changed to the Beacon Presbyterian Church. He became associated with Rev. Francis Robbins, D.D., who looked chiefly after the finances while Mr. Marr attended largely to the routine work of the pulpit and parish. Together they planned the large organization it afterwards became. Thus from a membership of only sixty-five and a Sunday school of four hundred and ninety-seven, meeting in what had been a mill, the work grew in eleven years into a church membership of six hundred and fifty and the Sunday school of one thousand and ninety-six, meeting in a large and handsome building, with rooms for sewing classes, cooking classes, night schools and a free medical dispensary.

He resigned his position as co-pastor of the Beacon Church in 1893 and supplied vacant churches whenever he was called upon. When death came he was at his house near Point Pleasant, N. J. On June 3d, 1895, "he had risen from the table with the remark that he felt in perfect health, and he submitted to the summons, which came in about an hour after, with a protest, saying that there were some things he wished to accomplish before going. But when it became apparent that the summons was peremptory and a final call from above, he acquiesced, saying that he was ready if it were the Father's will, and that it was in accordance with his wish to die in this speedy manner. After giving a few words of consolation to his wife and of admonition to his boy, he turned over and breathed his last." "The rapid action of occult pneumonia alone accounted for the sudden collapse of his vigorous constitution." He thus passed away apparently in the midst of health.

Mr. Marr was a man of a strong physical constitution and an iron will. He worked through Summer's heat and Winter's cold. "He never took a vacation in his twenty-eight years of service nor missed an engagement through illness." He was self-denying, thinking but little of his own needs but much of his people's requirements among whom he worked. Capable of filling a lucrative position in the mercantile world, he gave his talents to the Lord's cause, receiving but small compensation in all of his fields of labor. He was a man of warm piety and decided character. He loved to preach the gospel and he was untiring in pastoral work, especially among the poor, the needy and the sick. From childhood his "characteristics were an indomitable will and energy, conscientiousness and courage; always cheerful, strictly honorable and having remarkable self-control." These characteristics he maintained throughout his life. No word of jealousy escaped his lips nor spirit of indictiveness showed itself in him. He was remarkably guarded in his statements about others. Socially he was genial and affable; his friendships were of the strongest. He was happily constituted so as to accommodate himself to his surroundings, and in his different fields of labor his circumstances were not always the most comfortable. He has finished his course as a true son of God and a faithful helper of man.

Minute adopted by the session on the death of Rev. James H. Marr:

It is with deep regret that we have heard of the sudden death of Rev. James H. Marr, the first pastor of this Church, at his home at Beacon-by-the-Sea, New Jersey, on June 3d, 1885.

We, as a session, desire to put on record our high regard for his Christian character, his deep piety, his earnest zeal for the Master's cause, and his love for all things which related to the Lord's kingdom. As the organizer of this Church, he worked with indomitable perseverance, courage and charity until he had developed it from a small mission church, to a self-supporting one. Its success is largely due to his ability, fidelity and discriminating judgment.

We realize that by his death this Church has lost a true friend and helper, and that the church at large has lost a faithful and zealous worker. We submissively bow in resignation to the All-wise Providence of God in thus removing from his earthly work one of His zealous followers.

We tender our sincere sympathy to his widow and family, and we offer our prayers for God's blessing and comfort.

We direct that a copy of this minute be sent to the family and that it be spread upon our records.

By order of the Session.

DAVID O. IRVING, Moderator.

WILLIAM S. MILLS, Clerk.

www.ingramcontent.com/pod-product-compliance
Lightning Source LLC
Chambersburg PA
CBHW031800090426
42739CB00008B/1094